THE BOOK OF CUTE SHAPES

THE BOOK OF CUTE SHAPES

ABOUT THIS BOOK

Learning about shapes is very important to young children. This will help them with a variety of skills such as creativity, geometry, sorting objects, and communication improvement. Also, learning about shapes at an early age provides a foundation for learning how to read and write. The super cute images in this book were designed to promote positive feelings and a fun learning experience. The book of cute shapes is sure to provide everyone with a pleasant time. What a fun way to learn!

CIRCLE

SQUARE

TRIANGLE

RECTANGLE

DIAMOND
(RHOMBUS)

OVAL

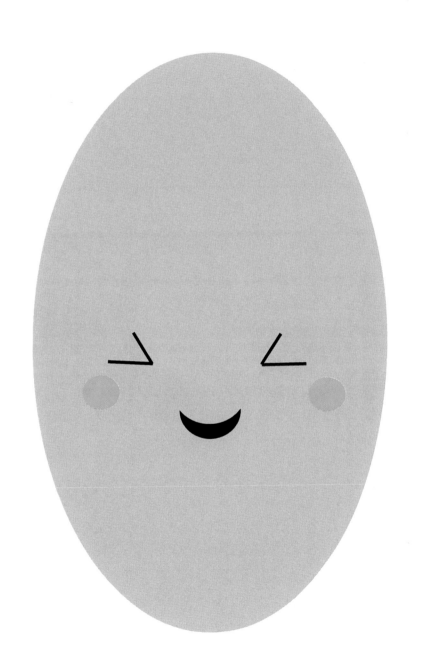

HEART

PENTAGON

HEXAGON

TRAPEZOID

PARALLELOGRAM

CROSS